A Look Inside

Bipolar

Disorder

A Look Inside Bipolar Disorder

One Woman's Story

By
Tracy Suzanne Green

E-BookTime, LLC
Montgomery, Alabama

A Look Inside Bipolar Disorder
One Woman's Story

Library of Congress Control Number: 2007925569

ISBN: 978-1-59824-511-0

First Edition
Published March 2007
E-BookTime, LLC
6598 Pumpkin Road
Montgomery, AL 36108
www.e-booktime.com

Introduction

My name is Tracy Green and I am twenty-eight years old. I am married to a wonderful young man named Dennis. Our fifth wedding anniversary is coming up. I have two beautiful and healthy boys, Joshua and Colin. They are four and two respectively. I am a stay at home mom which means I get to stay at home all day while others have to fight traffic to get to work. I also have two basset hounds named Samantha and Marty. My bills are all paid. I live in a two bedroom, brick house with a two car garage and have great neighbors. I am extremely close to my parents and brother and I have a few very special friends who would do just about anything for me. Seems like I have the perfect life right? Read on to find out.

My current diagnosis which came merely two years ago is bipolar disorder. I write this book in hopes of reaching others who have felt the pain that comes along with this mental illness. It is a terrible illness that destroys lives, those of the one that have it, and those that are affected by the person that has the disorder. I write this for the millions of others who have this disorder. This is my story and there are millions of others probably very similar. It is my hope that more people come forward to share their story. I know it would make me feel better to know that I am not alone, as I often do feel.

It is important for me to point out that I do not write this book with the intention of gaining sympathy that is not my intention. I truly want to spread awareness of how difficult it can be living with this disorder and hopefully shed a little light on what it is all about. I currently am doing well, am on the proper medications, and will soon be entering therapy. However, for years and years as you will see, I was in complete denial that there was anything wrong with me. I could have felt better much sooner if I had just admitted to myself that there was something wrong. So, if you are reading this and find yourself with similar symptoms, please seek help, you will feel much better, I know that I do.

Chapter One

I guess the real story starts back to high school…..I think that is when my illness began. I did not know it at the time, but the symptoms were all there. I guess to illustrate a story would be ideal. I was dating a young man named Jesus. Boy, did I take some jokes for that one. "You're going out with Jesus?" they would say. Anyways he was in a school play one night. After his performance I wanted him to come hang out with me. However, he preferred to go to the drama club party. Now, to the normal person, this would probably have been fine, but not to me. I came home with my parents humiliated. When my parents asked what was wrong, I flew into a rage. We are not talking about a few tears; I mean a full blown rage. I went ballistic. My head was racing and I could not get a hold of myself. I began screaming at the top of my lungs to my parents. "It's none of your fucking business!" I was saying. Along with, "I hate you and wish you never brought me to that stupid play." I remember even trying to get out the door, and shoving my mom out of the way. My dad came up behind me and kicked me to the floor. I will never forget his words. He said, "Are you on drugs?" The truth being I needed to be on drugs, but not the recreational kind. No, I needed to be medicated, but hindsight is twenty/twenty they say. I was a wreck and could not understand how Jesus, my boyfriend not the savior, could do this to me. "What is wrong with me?" was all I could ask myself. That is pretty much all I remember from that night. What I did not know was that this was the first incident of many that would show evidence that there was more going on than I had realized.

There were also times when I would go into a rage on my friends. Looking back, I often wonder what they thought as I was screaming into their faces. One time it involved my friend Amber. She had come to my house one night very upset about her boyfriend and her. So, I told my friend that was visiting at the time that I had to speak to Amber and calm her down and asked my friend to leave.

So, I comforted Amber because she was hysterical. Finally she calmed down and we both decided that he was not worth all these tears.

The next day, her boyfriend showed up at our lunch table. I went crazy. I could not believe that he was sitting at our table after he had hurt Amber just the night before to the point that she showed up at my house hysterical. What I did not know was that he had sincerely apologized to Amber and that they had patched things up. I was furious. You see, there should not have been a reason for me to be so furious with Amber. I would not even sit at the same lunch table as them. It was one of our biggest fights. I remember screaming at her in front of the whole cafeteria, "How can you forgive him?" And I also had a few choice names for her boyfriend as well. You would have thought I would be happy for them, but there was something in me that flew me into a rage. I remember I did not even eat my lunch. All I could see was red. Along with this story, there were countless times when I would go into a rage on the phone with my friend Jill. I remember that my parents would be in the other room yelling for me to calm down. Jill certainly never deserved the wrath that I gave her, none of my friends did. However, I am happy to say that I have some very forgiving and special friends. Amber, Jill, and I are still friends to this day despite my bipolar disorder and its ramifications.

My next serious relationship was with a young man named Steve. Did I fail to mention that I had to be in a relationship or my life was completely worthless? I went from one relationship to another thinking that this person would save me. In fact, I started at seventeen using sex as a way to solve this problem in my head. My head would hurt and I did not know why. I do not mean a headache. I mean there was no way of shutting off my brain. Every time my mother would suggest that I go talk to a counselor, I would fly off into another rage telling her that she was the one that belonged in therapy. I think that I have hurt her to the point now that she probably will go into therapy. Going back to my brain hurting, what I mean is that my thoughts would race at night and sleep was never easy. Honestly, even now that I have been diagnosed with bipolar disorder, sleep still is a stress and so are my ever racing thoughts that occur. What a vicious cycle, no sleep so my thoughts race, my thoughts race, so no sleep. What I wouldn't give to make this all go away, but this is life and the only way to get better is to talk it out and take my medication. I'm digressing though, I was talking about Steve.

Steve was a wonderful boyfriend. Extremely caring and thoughtful and always treated me like a princess. He knew something was wrong with me because there were times when I would discuss suicide. I never attempted when I was with Steve, but often thought about it. I think throughout our whole relationship I was depressed. The question is why was I so depressed? Here I had this wonderful boyfriend who I thought at the time I was going to marry and I was depressed. It is not as if I was doing poorly in college either. My grades were great and I was involved in several clubs. Sure makes perfect sense doesn't it? Everything is going great in my life so I feel terrible and suicidal. That is the crazy thing about the low side of bipolar, everything can be going great and yet you feel depressed. Go figure. After about two years of dating Steve, it was obvious that Steve could not fill this void in my head, or save me. So, I went on to find someone else.

This time it was someone that I worked with. His name was Stewart. Hey, he was someone different. Maybe this time, this relationship would save me from myself. Maybe this relationship would take away my pain. I was simply kidding myself. I think that if being in a relationship could fix problems than most of the world's problems would go away, but that is just silly. I tried sex again, but that did not help. Nothing helped. Every relationship I was in we would discuss marriage. That was another topic that I used to defer my pain. I had the absurd idea that putting a ring on my finger would save me from my pain. Again, I was kidding myself. How could entering into the sacred sacrament of marriage help me feel better or make racing thoughts go away? If anything the new stress of being married would intensify my situation and make it worse, but I did not know that.

My grandmother on my mother's side passed away during this time. I was a junior in college at this point. I remember why Stewart and I broke up. I did not want him to come to the funeral. Sure he would have been a comfort, but I did not want this event to be the time that I introduced him to my family. He flipped out on me and could not understand why I did not want him there. The night before we buried my grandmother, I went into another rage. My poor mom was about to bury her mom and there I was being selfish carrying on about Stewart. I will never forget hurting my mom that night, not physically, but emotionally. I could just not get a hold of my emotions. What was I going to do if Stewart broke up with me which he threatened to do? I was going to have to be alone. Little did I realize that this would have been the best thing for me at the time? Perhaps I could take time off from dating, learn about myself, and heal from this awful pain. Get out of the dating scene for a minute and take a break? Like that was going to happen. No, for some reason I needed these relationships even though they did not help my problem at all. In fact, during most of them it was evident that I had a problem with my mood swings, but would I admit that? Hell no.

Chapter Two

I should explain the type of pain that I had and still have. I do not have physical pain with this disorder, only mental anguish. Sometimes I think I would rather break my arm or leg than deal with this mental pain. It's the kind of pain that tells you to hurt yourself, tells you that you are worthless and makes you want to just stay in bed and let the world pass you by. However, you can't do that. You have to get up. For me, there are days when it is such a struggle to begin my day. The last thing I want to do is go get my children their cheerios and juice, and not to mention their fluoride. When my four years old asks me, "How was your night's sleep Mommy?" I lie and tell him how great it was. In reality, I could not fall asleep because my mind kept replaying scenes from a recent movie that I saw or that all I could think about was how could I painlessly kill myself. But I lie and tell him that my night sleep was terrific as I gulp down three cups of coffee to try to wake up.

You see, one thing about bipolar that I am noticing is that it has a ripple affect. One problem affects another part of your life, and so on and so on. I have racing thoughts, so I cannot sleep, so I cannot wake up, so my kids get hungry, and I am late bringing my one son to school, so then I feel guilty. Oh guilt! That is an emotion that should be written into the title of the illness. Not a day goes by when I do not feel guilt. Guilt for how I feel, for what I said, for what I did not say, for what I did, for what I did not do, etc.... I joke that I was raised Catholic and that is why I always have guilt, but that is not the truth. Guilt is like a parasite on your heart. It takes a hold of you and does not let go. I still have guilt about things I have done, but it is getting better, slowly but surely. Do not let guilt stop you from pursuing your dreams. Do not let guilt stop you from still seeking help. Forgive yourself. Personally, I feel that forgiving yourself is one of the hardest things on this planet to do, but if you can do it, then is a wonderful thing. When you hurt other people like friends or family, you cannot always be forgiven. However, you can forgive you.

Chapter Three

Okay, so I digressed again, this time for a while but it's worth explaining what type of pain goes along with this illness. So Stewart and I broke things off. I went back to college and this time had some random hook-ups which in my book just mean kissing. I know too many others it means much more, but not in this case. I was kissing these random guys to try to make my sadness go away. I think if kissing was a cure for depression, it would put a lot of drug companies out of business. Even my roommate was a little worried about me when I ended up hooking up with her brother's friend. I did not even like the guy, but he was there and I was lonely and depressed so I went for it. He never called me and not that I expected him to. Why don't boys call when they say they will? But, that's a whole other book. At this point I needed to find another boyfriend because after all it had been about a month or so.

When I went home for Easter break that junior year I decided that it was time for another boyfriend. Who would be the prince charming this time to sweep me off my feet and save me from myself? This time I decided to date someone else that I used to work with. His name was Mark and he was five years older than me. Age did not matter; all that mattered was that I could use him to try to feel better. Wow, that is the first time I admitted that to myself. Yes, I used these guys. Sure I liked them to a point, but mainly I liked the attention. I liked the idea that I was not alone in this world. God knows if I was not in a relationship than I was nothing. That is the way I probably would feel to this day if my husband and I divorced which has almost happened on several occasions due to my bipolar and its ramifications. So, getting back to Mark, we dated for about seven months. I remember that my illness really began to show during this time but of course I did not do anything about it. Every time we would have sex I would cry myself to sleep afterwards. The truth is I do not know why really. Possibly because even sex was not cutting it. It was not taking the edge off of my racing thoughts and thoughts of worthlessness. In fact, it began to deepen them. That did not stop me though, I continued on my strange trail of trying to find a cure for something that I did not know that I had.

Looking back, how could I not know that I was sick? Maybe I knew deep inside but just did not want to admit it to myself. I mean, I was an educated girl and I could not see the signs of bipolar? I must have been in deep denial, or a complete fool. I will choose that I was in denial. Denial is such a strong defense mechanism. I honestly thought, despite all my ups and downs, that I was fine. I had pushed down the idea that I was sick so far down that it had no room to breathe. Even though I would have thoughts of suicide and even though there were times I could not control my thoughts, yeah sure, I was fine. No problems here.

I knew that I did not love Mark and that he did not love me so I ended it. Hardly a tear or two was shed on the ending of that relationship. Hey at least it was not some drown out, dramatic, break-up. No, we pretty much had breakfast together one February morning and I had decided that our relationship was not working.

I remember there was a parents' weekend at my school during this semester. My parent's drove the three hour drive as they did every parents weekend just to be with me. Of course, there had to be an incident. It had to do with where we were going to eat lunch that first afternoon that they arrived. They just wanted to eat in the cafeteria. How could this be I thought? I was being selfish. You see, I was so tired of eating in the cafeteria that I went into another full blown rage about the situation. I wanted to eat somewhere off campus, but they were hungry and just wanted to eat at the closest facility. Of course they were hungry, they had just driven three hours to come and see me. Any other young adult probably just would have complained a little and then dropped the issue. But not me. No, I decided that this was my chance to tell my parents just how cheap they were and nasty they were being making me eat in the cafeteria. Honestly, looking back, the cafeteria at my school actually had excellent food. I knew this, but hey I did not want to miss a chance to scream at the top of my lungs at my parents which

I did for about a half hour. I will never forget my dad giving me the finger and walking off campus to my apartment. I was so miserable and felt horribly guilty after my mood swing subsided. All they wanted was to get something to eat in the quickest amount of time because of their hunger, but I failed to see it their way I guess. However, it is hard to be rational when you are in a full blown rage. You see red. You only see things your way and you cannot figure out how people cannot just go with what you are saying. In sum, you are being completely selfish.

Chapter Four

It was halfway into my senior year in which I ended things with Mark. Like after every other relationship, I wasn't happy until I was in the next one. Thank goodness for Tony then I guess you could say. He was in the band with my friend's boyfriend. He got me to start smoking and drink loads of caffeine. Boy, he was good for my soul. A real prize winner. Again, I thought this was the one just like every other boyfriend. I was thrilled when I got into a graduate school that was near where he lived. I am not saying I would not have gone to this graduate school anyway, but he certainly sealed the deal. It was not all bad, and Tony definitely had his good points. It was only a couple weeks after getting my bachelor's and moving home to be near him that he broke things off. I remember the night vividly. My friend Amber was having a bunch of people over. I could tell right away when I got there that he wished I had stayed home because he just wanted time with his friend. However, I was there. I went into one of my fits when I saw that he was not happy to see me. I ran away to a local firehouse and stayed on their steps crying my eyes out waiting for him to come. Another smart idea I had. Run away to somewhere late at night in a bad neighborhood. Not one of my brighter ideas. I was waiting for Tony to come. He never did.

Finally, Amber found me and made me go back to the house with her. Tony never said anything to me when I walked in the door. Feeling humiliated, I wanted to die and I mean literally. I went upstairs and Amber gave me some sort of pill to calm down. God, I wish it worked. I lay on her bed and just kept saying, "I just want to die." Finally Tony came upstairs and hearing my profession of wanting to die told me that he could not do this anymore. I went ballistic and begged him not to leave me. After all, it was me that left relationships and I could not have someone abandon me. I cannot say that I blame him though. I may have even done the same thing if the shoe were on the other foot. How could I expect him to handle a girlfriend who wanted to die all the time? Also, who would want to be with someone who wanted to die all the time?

It is probably important that I go back and discuss my senior year. There were other things going on which pointed to bipolar which I did not know until now. When I would go home, there were times I would go down the shore to Atlantic City with my dad. Only I would not just gamble twenty or thirty dollars. Little did my dad know, but I would hit up the credit card and waste about two-hundred dollars which may not sound like a lot, but it was for me at the time. Gambling was and still is another way in which I try to make myself feel better. I use it to block out feelings of worthlessness. It is also a way I try to battle my loneliness. There is something about sitting with a bunch of strangers that I like and that makes me feel less alone-go figure. It has now progressed into such a terrible addiction that I have probably lost close to ten-thousand dollars over the past couple years. It is the casino that I go to when I am feeling lost and blue and just plain worthless. Sure, makes perfect sense doesn't it? Go drive down to a dangerous city by yourself, have too much to drink, lose tons of money that your husband earned, get depressed that you lost the money, drive home sleepy and buzzed, and feel guilty the whole ride home. Oh, and what is waiting for you when you get home? Usually an angry husband is waiting at the door. Then I have to profess how sorry I am and how I will never do it again. It honestly has nothing to do with the money. I would probably feel just as bad about myself if I came home with a million dollars. It is about the rush, the rush of winning a lot, usually just to lose it all back. It is that rush that I crave. Oh the joys of having bipolar! I am still not sure if when I go down if it is because I am feeling manic or it is when I am depressed. My doctor calls what I have sometimes "mixed episodes" so maybe that is it. Anyways, to make a long story short, I have a gambling addiction that I think resulted from my bipolar disorder. I know that they are related, but God I wish that they were not. Just this past week, I probably went down the shore four times, and have of course lost all of my money. I have even sold my wedding rings for a lousy hundred dollars now that is depressing.

Along with all the monetary things I have lost, I have nearly lost something especially sacred—my marriage and my kids.

Getting back to my senior year of college, this was an especially difficult year for me. I used to be excellent at giving speeches. Well, this one time, I got all panicked in front of the entire class. I started shaking. I should point out too that during every class after that I would have panic attacks. I would be sitting in the middle of class and I could not breathe. This was not from having bipolar, but it certainly depressed me. I got so depressed because school was one of the one thing that I excelled at, and now that too was being taken away from me. Therefore, I was losing my mind due to this disorder and my physical control. My heart would race, my hands would shake, and I would just want to run out of the classroom. But, I applied to graduate schools anyways because that is what you did if your major was speech pathology/audiology.

Chapter Five

Before I discuss graduate school, I want to discuss a little more in depth my college years. They were definitely not all bad. In fact, I met two wonderful girls who are still very dear friends to this day. I was in both of their weddings and they were in mine. My first three years of college actually went pretty smoothly. Sure, I would have my depressed moments and manic moments. However, I would explain my depressed moments to my roommate at the time as a result of missing home. When I was manic, my friends tended to like it because I was so up and happy. They liked that side to Tracy. It was not until my senior year when my life started getting very complicated and the bipolar starting showing its ugly head. My roommate would go home a lot and I remember feeling so alone, even though I could go hang out with my friends. I would sit in that lonesome apartment and just bawl my eyes out. I never told her this to this day and she will never know unless she reads this book. I would lie there, on my apartment floor, just crying my eyes out because I felt so alone. What was stopping me from going to my friend Julie's dorm or my friend Meghan's house? To this day I do not know the answer to that. You see, I think with bipolar, when you are depressed, you are extremely irrational, and it is the same when you are manic. It would have been rational to call up my friends, but those depressive thoughts are just so strong that they overtake your thinking.

When I started graduate school, it was not long before these panicky feelings arose. In fact, just being at the orientation was disturbing enough. I should point out that at this time I began dating my future husband named Dennis. He is a whole other chapter though in himself. So, I got through two weeks of graduate school somehow and just could not deal with the panic attacks. I made the painstaking decision to quit graduate school. I will never forget the disappointment on my parent's faces. Little did they know that their little girl was suffering from an illness that she did not have control of. I stopped graduate school in September of 2005 and to make my life even more complicated, got pregnant a month later.

As if I did not feel guilt enough for quitting graduate school due to these awful panic attacks, the guilt of being pregnant before marriage was devastating. Not only did I let myself down, but I let all my family down as well. How could I get pregnant prior to having a ring on my finger and standing in front of a priest? I was raised Catholic and always believed that I would wait to have sex until after I as married. Well, that did not happen. It was all too much for me and my depression worsened.

If I may digress a little bit, there was a point around this time when I sought out help due to the concern given by Dennis and my parents about how low I was feeling. It was September 11th, how could I forget that date. Dennis came over early that morning after one of the towers had been struck, and despite this awful world event, they still wanted to take me to the doctors. So, off we went to see my nurse practitioner. Of course she asked me one of the main questions, "Have you thought of hurting yourself?" to which I honestly replied "yes." To her credit she told me, Dennis and my father that I was in crisis and needed to go to the hospital. Once again I felt guilt. The World Trade Center Towers were demolished and I was being treated for my little problem.

When we got to the hospital it was obvious that everyone's attention was on the television. I felt like an idiot answering the questions from the triage doctor. I was assuming that he thought I must have been the most selfish person in the world. People were dying, being burned alive, and there I was telling him how depressed I was. Not much came out of that visit to the hospital. The truth is they should have kept me overnight and put me on some sort of medication, but they did not. They simply had some counselor talk to me and give me tips on how to handle when I was feeling down. Boy that was a waste of time. I should have been at a church praying, but instead I listened to some novice counselor tell me what signs to look for when I am feeling low. I felt ridiculous as we left that hospital. Nothing good came out of the whole ordeal unfortunately.

Chapter Six

Since I was not in graduate school, I got a job working as a program assistant for a special needs school. This was a very positive experience for me. I learned so much about myself and what I loved doing which was helping people. Most of the kids were in wheelchairs and had multiple disabilities. I drew closest to the children who were the sickest. I will explain how that ties in with what I eventually would like to do later. My days there were mostly happy ones and I really felt at ease working with those kids along with the adults at the adult program. Along with being a teacher assistant there were times when I was a speech assistant and got to work alongside the speech pathologist. I really enjoyed this and found it quite rewarding. I really felt at home in that school and felt completely comfortable with all the children and adults.

The only thing that bothered me was that people were always bringing up the fact that I could get such a better job since I had a degree. Every time someone would say something along those lines it would make me feel guilty and bad about myself. Once I was a long term substitute for about seven weeks and I just could not handle the pressure. It was too much. I could not breathe during the day. Everyone told me what a great job I was doing, but I could just not handle the pressure. I wanted to go back to being just an assistant. That was about all I could handle with nobody counting on me, nobody depending on me, just a simple assistant.

The question that I have to ask myself is, "If I am really good at something, why do I feel the need to bring it to an end?" That is something that I just do not understand. This is the first time I am following through with something, writing this book. Everyone always enjoys my writing, and gosh darn it; I am going to go through with this. I am finally feeling better which I will discuss later, and therefore I am going to follow through with some of my dreams. I did not know until now, but this is a dream of mine, writing this book and getting it published. If I could help just one person, than I have accomplished something. It is also extremely therapeutic to sit down and write down all of your thoughts and feelings and I would recommend it to anyone going through something.

It should be mentioned that I am extremely hard on myself and hardly ever give myself any credit. I often wonder if this goes along with the disorder, never feeling good about myself or what I have accomplished. It has to be linked with depression. Another one of those vicious cycles—I feel depressed so I will not feel good about things I have done. I do good things but feel worthless so will not allow myself to feel good. Oh the joys that comes along with being bipolar. One of these days I am going to be proud of something I have accomplished. I am going to look at what I have done, and say, "Yes, I did that and damn it is good."

Where was I? Oh yes, I had gotten pregnant out of wedlock. It was not an easy pregnancy either because of my mood swings which were heightened when I was pregnant. It is amazing that Dennis stayed with me during this time. I could not say that I would have blamed him if he got on the nearest bus out of town. The upside is that I had a beautiful ten pound (yes, he was c-section) boy named Joshua. He is the light of my life now when there seems to be only darkness. Many days it is Joshua that keeps me going. His heart is a big as the ocean and I do not know where my life would be without him. In a strange way having Joshua saved my life. I still continued to have terrible highs and lows, but I knew that I had to fight it because the stakes were higher now. I had this adorable boy to take care of, and he was mine. He is now four years old and is finishing up his second year of preschool. He really excels in school and I know that he will do great in the years ahead. Joshua is a social butterfly and the girls love him. He will definitely be a heart breaker when he grows up. No, he will not be the kind to break hearts, he is too kind. He will probably marry his high school sweetheart, but I digress.

Chapter Seven

So Dennis and I were living in sin with Joshua in a cute average sized one bedroom apartment. Another thing I had to feel guilty over, living with my fiancé. We did not want to have some sort of shot-gun wedding. No, we wanted the whole thing, ceremony, reception, dancing, you name it. So, there I was with a newborn planning our wedding, talk about stress. It was during this time that I started to take my trips down the shore by myself to go gambling. It was not bad at first and Dennis did not even mind. I never lost a whole lot and I was working so it was not like I was losing Dennis's money. So, these trips were in some respects not nearly as bad as they are now. I even would go with friends at times, not now though. There were even times when Dennis would go down with me and we would walk the boards and then he would let me go gamble for a little bit. Wow, what a different time that was. One time we even stayed overnight at Harrah's casino. I think hell would half to freeze over for that to happen now. Anyways, it was during this time that was the beginning of my horrible addiction. It was during this time that I started to use gambling as an escape for my underlining problem—bipolar disorder.

After I had Joshua I decided to talk to my doctor about my depressed moods. She felt I had mild depression (I wish) and she put me on Zoloft. I took that for several years. Unfortunately, if you have bipolar disorder than anti-depressants can actually make you feel worse. I should have mentioned to her that I would go out gambling, this would have been a red flag that there was more going on here, but I was too ashamed. So, when I would go see her of course I was feeling worse and worse and she just kept upping the dosage. It never helped.

We had a very nice wedding on October 12th, 2002. I have to say that I was proud of all the things that I did for the wedding like making the invitations, booking the DJ, making the centerpieces, and more. Everything came together. The best part being that I married the most amazingly forgiving man on this entire planet. He has been to hell and back with me and has stayed by my side. We never really had a honeymoon but hope to someday. How could we? We had a four month old to take care of at home. Nevertheless, I will never forget that day and how happy I was. God I wish I could feel that good all the time and never get depressed. What I wouldn't give to bottle that happiness that I felt on my wedding day and just pour it over me on days like today when all I can think about is death and how I want to be with the angels.

Very shortly after we were married, we moved into the house that we live in now. It is a very cute house, Cape Cod model. We have been here close to five years. I continued to work at the special needs school. In fact, I worked there close to four years. I have been out of work for two years and have been a stay at home mom. There were several times at work when it was evident that I had more than depression. I worked under this teacher that was extremely picky and demanding. After being in her class for several months, I became pregnant with my second son Colin. Anyways, she said some comment to me one day about working with a certain child and I screamed at her, "I am pregnant; there is no way I am going to go near that child!" Another time while working with this certain teacher, she said something and it set me off. "You are so fucking picky!" I told her. Then I became hysterical and ran up to my boss's office pleading to be put into another room which never happened. The truth is to this day I do not know what made me so upset. Driving home I could not believe that I had shown my rage to someone outside of my family. The next day, feeling terribly guilty, I apologized profusely to the teacher and my boss. They thought nothing of it, but I knew deep down that I needed help.

Another time I had an incident with another teacher. I should point out that during this pregnancy I did stay on my medication, but it was not helping. Of course it was not. I was taking something that was actually making me feel and act worse. One morning one of the teachers looked at me and said, "Wow, you are big." Now, I know I was hormonal at the time; of course I was because I was eight months pregnant. However, my reaction went beyond that of being able to blame it on hormones. I yelled at her, and I mean yelled. I was in a manic state; everything pissed me off, especially a comment like that. She never talked to me again and I cannot say that I blamed her.

Yes, there were several occasions while working at that school that pointed towards bipolar, but why in the world would I want to admit that? What was there to gain by admitting that I could not control my anger at times and at times I was so low I wanted to veer off the side of the road and be left for dead? The truth being that there was everything to gain I just did not know it at the time.

Chapter Eight

So, eventually I stopped working at this school. My son Colin had colic really bad. All he would do for hours on end is cry. One day I was at work, the babysitter called. I could hear Colin crying in the background. She called me at work and said, "What do I do about this?" And it was at that moment that I decided to become a full time mother. I told my boss that I just could not leave him alone, and that he needed me. Luckily, they did not give me any problems, and I did not even have to give them two weeks. I would be lying if I said that I do not miss that job. The children that I worked with were so inspiring to me and working with them made me a better person. The people that I worked with were amazing too and I am happy to say that I keep in touch with many of them. They understood my decision and many of them wished they could do the same thing. My husband is in the Army and he makes enough so that I am able to stay home. In that respect, I feel truly blessed.

I think it is important for me to be completely honest in this book which is why I should discuss what happened last night before I go on with my story. It was like any other night, my thoughts were racing and I had to get away. This time the urge was too much and I had to leave the house. What is it about getting in my car and driving places that somehow makes me feel better? I do not know the answer to that but wish that I did. So I told my husband that I had to go for a drive. He asked me if I was depressed to which I lied and told him no. Of course I was depressed or I would not have entered that car and drove miles on end to a casino in Pennsylvania. I hardly had any money, but I lost the money that I did have.

When I came home I took it out on my husband. I went into a rage. See, I am on medication and supposedly pretty level, but despite that I still have my moments. So, I came home at 2:00 in the morning and decided it was a good time to pick a fight with my husband. The poor guy, all he wanted to do was sleep. I asked him if I could have six buck to buy a pack of cigarettes. When he refused, I went ballistic. "I hate you; I want a divorce, fuck you!" These were some of my eloquent words. I even told him that I wanted a divorce. When I finally settled down I went to sleep. This is how unbelievable my husband is. I woke up to find a cup of coffee next to my bed, my medication, a beautiful letter Dennis had written me, and the money I wanted for cigarettes. Talk about an incredible man. There I was only a few hours prior cursing him out and he decides to make everything better when it should have been me apologizing profusely. God, I really am blessed to have Dennis in my life. I could not ask for a more supportive, forgiving man to have in my life. So, this all just happened within the last twenty-four hours, which just goes to show that this sickness does not end simply because you are medicated. You will still have your moments which are a bitch, but it is the truth.

Chapter Nine

If I could take a magic pill that would make this all go away, believe me I would. Of course, what I have to realize is that this is something I will have to deal with the rest of my life. However, despite last night, I have started to gain control of some of my emotions. Unfortunately, I will be ridden with guilt over last night for oh, about a week or so. It is not even as though there is someone there trying to make me feel guilty, I just am terrible at forgiving myself. It is not an easy feat especially when you make such poor decisions. I guess part of me could blame it on the illness, but I choose not to. I believe that I always have a choice. I have to hold myself accountable for my actions and not simply say, "Well, I have bipolar disorder." It is this kind of thinking will get me nowhere fast in life.

Where was I? Ah yes, I had decided to become a stay at home mom, and still am to this day. It has it's good points and bad points I guess you could say. What I miss the most is being around all my coworkers. Do not get me wrong I do not miss working with that obsessive compulsive teacher; however I do miss my coworkers and especially the kids. I tell you, some of those kids will brighten your darkest day, and they force you to realize that you take your life for granted. If you see a child, hooked up to a feeding tube, on a ventilator, in a wheelchair and they are still smiling, then what in the world do you have to be upset about? In a way, it was therapeutic for my soul and I guess I miss that aspect of the job the most.

However, let me tell you about my job now which I consider the best job in the world. I get to wake up and make breakfast for my two adorable boys. One of them eats cheerios every morning, and the other always wants oatmeal. Of course, juice is mandatory at every breakfast. Then we usually watch cartoons and/or play until it is time for me to drop my oldest son Joshua off at preschool. Colin of course comes along and enjoys going down the steps into

Joshua's classroom, we like to count them. It makes me sad to think that he is almost at the age where he will be starting school.

A few months ago Dennis and I were trying to make a third baby. However, it was not in God's plan for our lives and I now know why. The medication that is working for me cannot be taken if one is pregnant. More selfish as it may sound, I would rather feel good and act normal than to bring another child into this world. Plus, God only knows what would happen if I were to go off the medication all together. What would happen for those nine long months? Would I even make it? Would my children and husband suffer? It is almost too much to think about. Therefore, Dennis and I have stopped trying to get pregnant. This saddens me, because I really did want a third child. It is not that I wanted to try for a girl, as many of you will probably think, I would have been completely happy having another boy. Who knows it may have in fact been easier. We even had started turning the basement into a third bedroom. Now, every time I see the started construction, it breaks my heart. However, we are going to go ahead and turn part of the basement into a room for Joshua so he can have a separate bedroom. Again, God only knows though what would happen if I went off my medication. Sadly, it is just not in the cards for me to have a third.

Getting back to staying at home, after we drop Joshua off at preschool Colin and I head home usually to play while I watch Regis and Kelly on the television. Sometimes I even stop at Dunkin Donuts and pick up something to snack on while I watch my morning television. Sometimes during this time Colin takes a nap and I get to have time all to myself which usually involves going on the computer to catch up on emailing or writing letters to friends. Or to be perfectly honest, sometimes I take a little nap myself.

Around noon is when we pick up Joshua from preschool. Again, Colin enjoys going down the steps and counting them as we do. Joshua is usually finishing up a puzzle when we come in the classroom. His teacher and her assistant are very nice. Luckily they have not said anything to me to set me off just yet. One never know though, it could be tomorrow, but God forbid. So, we drive home and Joshua tells me about his day at school. His worry is always whether or not lunch is ready and I usually have it all ready for the two of them. It is almost always peanut butter and jelly, they love it. After lunch I let Joshua watch television while Colin plays. I try to do some cleaning each day and laundry if it needs to be done. Before you know it, Dennis is home from work.

Chapter Ten

So, you see, my days are nice and relaxing, you would think. Then why do I get so blue at times? Why do I feel as though my life is worthless and meaningless? There are no answers as to why I feel that way. When I am not depressed I tell myself what an incredible thing I am doing raising these two boys and being there for them. However, other days, I am not so optimistic. I tell my husband that I do not do enough and that I am worthless. You see, there are days in fact when it is difficult to even get out of bed. Yes, getting out of bed is a task in itself. Getting my children their cheerios and oatmeal is difficult for me. Driving my son to preschool is the furthest thing from what I want to do. Yes, these are the days that I dread and I never know how I am going to feel in the morning. Dennis always reassures me that what I am doing is very important. God, I love him. Where would I be without Dennis in my life?

We met when I was seventeen and he was only sixteen. He was a friend of a friend. I will never forget our first phone conversation; we talked for about four hours. God, he could make me laugh and he still does. We dated for a bit but we were better off as friends. We kept in touch even when I was in college and he was in the army. When he got back from his time in South Korea, I asked him to my brother's wedding to which he agreed to go. I can honestly say that I had the night of my life. We danced almost the entire night and he was a great date. He even videotaped the wedding for my brother Matthew and sister-in-law Stacy. From then on we have been together.

Dennis understands my bipolar in a way that other people do not. He can tell just by the sound of my voice if I am having a low. By "having a low" I mean that I am depressed and am trying to fight my way out of it. Dennis probably takes the brunt of my disorder the most. He is the one who has to make sure that the children are okay when I up and leave and go anywhere but home. Dennis is the one waiting for me when I make it home from the casino half lit. Of course, I cannot say he is always happy at that point, but he always ends up forgiving me. The man is a saint. He has gone to doctors with me. Dennis is there when I am so depressed that I scream, "I just want to die" and "Why can't God just take me?" He is without a doubt the most forgiving man I have ever met and I just do not think he realizes how much I love him.

Going back to when I am feeling low, there is another downside to when I am feeling depressed. I have no desire to do anything, which means if my husband simply wants to go out for ice cream than I cannot bring myself to do it. In fact, just this past week I had to force myself to go to a movie with Dennis. He wants, as he should, alone time with me usually out of the house. I do not know why it is so difficult for me to get motivated to do things when I am feeling this way. If I do force myself to get out one of two things might happen. The first being that I get there and then have to leave because I am feeling that depressed. The second, which fortunately happens more commonly, is I will get to the place and I will get out of my funk, and I will be able to enjoy myself. Sometimes you have to force yourself to do what you do not want to do to realize that you wanted to do it after all. Am I confusing you yet?

About a year into staying home with my two sons, I saw an ad on television in which they were doing a study on those that had symptoms which were very similar to mine. So, I went to this place and right away they diagnosed me with bipolar disorder. It did not take long before they told me I would be perfect for a study they were conducting for those with bipolar. Now, you have to realize that up until this point, I had always thought I just had mild depression, so it was a little bit shocking to hear the words bipolar disorder.

However, I ended up going on a study for about eight months and then I finally took myself off of it. I was beginning to feel like a pin cushion from them sticking me all of the time. Plus, the medication they had me on was making me gain so much weight. Thankfully, I am on medication now that does not make me gain weight however, that was a superficial reason for me to stop the study. So, now I see a psychiatrist free of charge. He is great and only God know where I would be without him. It is easy for me to tell him how I am really feeling; there is no bullshitting with him.

Tonight Dennis and I went on a date. It was nice, his mom watched the boys so we could go bowling and go get something to eat. We had a fun time and it was much needed. We had not been out by ourselves in quite some time. Every time we go out just the two of us I see him in a different light. It is almost like I am seeing the young man that I first fell in love with. And it is fun to get dressed up for each other and realize just how beautiful and handsome we are. Everyone is beautiful in their own way. That is something that I am learning. Simply because we have faults and problems does not take away from the beauty that is within each and every one of us.

Chapter Eleven

I think that it is important to discuss the guilt that comes along with this disorder. I have guilt about everything. If I wake up late, I feel guilty. If I do not feel like I have spent enough time with my children, I am wracked with guilt. It has taken me years, but I think that I have finally forgiven myself for not completing graduate school. There are still times even four years later when I feel guilty about getting pregnant before I was married. Once again, I wish there was some magic pill that could take all this guilt away and I could just be free from it all. Of course, much of my guilt I bring on by myself. For instance, driving down the shore in the middle of the night to go gamble is something that I bring on myself. I really believe that despite feeling depressed or manic, there is always a choice of doing the right or wrong thing. Unfortunately, when you are feeling manic or depressed you often do not care about the consequences. You have no fear and you just go.

Once again, what an awful choice I have made time and time again. Driving down to a dangerous city, all by myself, losing my husband's money, drinking, talking to strangers and asking them for money, driving home with barely enough gas in the car, and then walking into the house to face an angry husband. Oh, and did I mention for that hour drive home I am beating myself up over the whole thing. There was one time when I walked the streets because I needed money so bad just so I could lose it on some silly slot machine. When I asked several random guys on the street, they told me they would give me the money if I just gave them a blow job. Thank the Lord, I never got that desperate or was that depressed or manic that I actually did it. That is something I do not think I could ever forgive myself for. That would have been a low I do not think I ever would have overcome and who knows what I would have done to myself then.

I should point out that there was a time when I attempted suicide. It is one thing to talk about it, but another thing to actually go through with it. My brother Matt was in town from Texas and I had just had my son Colin. Dennis and I wanted to go to the gym and Matt agreed to baby-sit. Now, looking back it was a bad idea. Matt had no children of his own and leaving him with a two and one week old was not the brightest idea. Once again though, I did not care about the consequences, I just knew that I had to get out of the house. I wanted to go into the whirlpool at the gym since I had just had a c-section I thought it would feel good. Well, once we were gone, my parents have called our house and were furious that we had left my brother all alone with the boys. We were not gone for that long but when we got home Matt told me about my parents. Well, I went into a rage. "What the fuck, it's not their business!" I said. Then I mistakenly directed my anger towards my brother and screamed at him. "Oh, what you said, they just left me with the boys" I said to him. For one of the first times in the time I have known my brother Matt, he got so angry with me that he walked out. It was freezing outside and Dennis pleaded with him to let him give Matt a ride home. He finally agreed, and I was humiliated. After I got the kids to bed I was alone. Dennis was still taking Matt to my parent's house and I was alone with a whole bunch of pills. I am not quite sure which kind of pill it was, but I do know it was one of my medications at the time. However, I swallowed about ten of them hoping never to wake up. I had let down my parents and my brother, and as silly as it seems, I wanted to die because of it. I was just so humiliated that I felt life was not worth living anymore. Obviously, my suicide attempt did not work because here I am today thank God.

Fortunately, that was my only real suicide attempt, but I cannot say that a day goes by that I think about ending my life, even though I am on the proper medication. That is not to say that I do not have good days, but many days I think I would be better off just being with God and having total peace. I often wonder if others ever feel the same way I do. A while ago I was saying to Dennis, "I just want to be with the angels." Could you imagine having a spouse that says that, he must get terrified in fact I know that he does. There have been times on my way back from the shore after gambling away all of our money that I have thought about veering off the side of the road and one time I lost control of the car and that almost happened. Knives are pretty interesting to me sometimes. I wonder what it would feel like to bleed out. I know this is pretty graphic, but one thing I told myself was that I would be completely honest in this book. It is actually extremely therapeutic.

Chapter Twelve

So, getting back to being a stay at home mom it has been about two years now since I made that decision. Like I was pointing out, there are good days and bad days. Days when I love that I am home with my kids and days when I would give anything to have a regular job. Of course, probably any stay at home mother feels that way at times. The kids are great. They like to play with Thomas the Tank Engine and do puzzles. Of course right now Colin is going through his terrible twos but that is to be expected. There are some kids in the neighborhood that Joshua likes to play with. For a four year old he is a popular kid. He goes to Church and they have a program for kids his age. He also goes to the gym with my husband and plays in the Kid's Club there. Colin also gets to go to these things which are great because it helps with their socialization skills. I do not think that my illness has had a negative impact on my children, as I try to hide when I am not feeling good. The only thing that I can think of that would have an affect on Joshua is when he sees me crying, which lately has happened a lot. He senses something is wrong with mommy but does not know what it is. Also, when I go down the shore for hours on end, when I get back he always asks where I was and tells me that he misses me. Alright, so my problems may have had somewhat of a negative affect on Joshua, however Colin is too young to notice.

Being a mom is something that comes somewhat naturally to me. The pregnancies were not easy, morning sickness is all day and does not end with the first trimester. Also, hemorrhoids are a bitch to have and so is acid reflux. However, the end result is what matters, and I got two incredible children. Something I do pride myself in (if you can believe it) is that I am a good mom. When they hurt, I hurt. All I want is for them to be happy, and if I could stay on my medication I would probably have two more, but that is not in the cards for me I do not think. They are my world and I would not give up being a mom for anything. I just wish they were not growing up so fast, but doesn't everyone say that? I can honestly say that we give them everything that they need and that they are having good childhoods. They have plenty of nice clothes, great food to eat, and tons of toys to play with. Yes, being a mom to these two blessings from God is something I am proud of even if one of them was born before I was married.

Chapter Thirteen

Today is a day when I would give anything just to get out of the house. I tried to do something positive and go get my hair trimmed, but they were all booked up. I have a gift certificate with them which is the only reason I would be able to get my hair cut. You see, my account is in the negative somewhere around $1400.00. It is all from being down the shore and asking my bank to transfer funds from an ING account that I did not even have. It would have been better if they did not even allow me to transfer those funds, funds that I did not even have but they did and I gambled it all away. Another time when driving home, I had thoughts of veering off the side of the road. Another time when I got so depressed that it was sitting with a bunch of strangers that took me to feel better. Go figure? I would give anything to have like $100.00 and get away from home even though there is a storm coming. That would not stop me though; nothing would if I had the money. Sadly, I have to take money out of my 401 K plan to cover the expenses of my gambling, now that is pathetic. That is money that I earned working at the special needs school and it took me four years to accumulate it, so what a waste. Probably would be cheaper if when I got depressed, I drank, just kidding. Sometimes you have to laugh, or you will just keep crying until your eyes burn and there are no tears left. I have been there and it is not fun.

So, I am hanging in there trying to do the right thing and stay home. Again, it is hard to do anything which is why it surprises me that I can sit here and write this. I think writing is very therapeutic for me. I should explain that I used to keep a journal. In fact, my good friend Kelly was asking me about that the other day. She said I should read back on my journals to get material for this book. I had to share with her that ironically I only wrote about the good things and covered up the bad things. Even in my own personal journal I was lying to myself, how amazing is that? Nobody but me would be reading these journals and yet I could not admit the truth even in them. The truth being that I was in terrible pain and chained down with sadness. But the truth was not even in them. I am finally at twenty-eight years old being honest with myself. It has certainly taken me a while, but better late than never I guess you could say.

Chapter Fourteen

Unfortunately, last night I was not able to just stay home. No, I went out driving and ended up at Harrah's Casino in Chester, Pennsylvania. It was even snowing at the time and the roads were terrible, but that did not stop me. No, there I was driving down the interstate with forty bucks in my wallet trying to strike it rich. So, I got there and within about two hours I had nothing left. I almost thought about asking some people for money, but this time I did not sink that low. Instead, I decided to drive home. I wanted to leave too because I knew the roads were going to get really bad, which they did. There I was driving home nearly veering off the road because of the ice. Was it worth it? Was driving forty minutes to some casino to lose forty bucks in the snow worth it? The answer being no, it was not worth it. When I came home surprisingly my husband was not upset, even though it was his forty bucks that I had blown. He was just happy that I was safe. Again, I have the most forgiving husband on the face of this planet.

A situation like last night, I would call manic. I had no regard for my safety or that of my family; I just knew I had to get away. This is what happens when I am manic, I have no regard for anyone else and I just do my own thing. It is like being in an extremely selfish state of mind. I think that I can find a new way to trick those machines into letting me win. God, what am I thinking? Today was not such a bad day though, I went to my parent's house so that the boys could play with their mom-mom and pop-pop. It was nice, and my mom even made an awesome chicken dinner. My parents are two of the most supportive people on this planet. They really are. They are always there for me when I need them, and even when I do not, but seriously, I do not know where I would be without them. My mom feels awful because mental illness runs in her side of the family. I try to tell her not to worry about it and that it could be worse. She still feels terrible that I have to go through these highs and lows as well as my dad.

Anyways, like I was saying today was a good day. I did not have any depressed feelings and I did not get manic and go drive somewhere. No, I stayed level all day which is a great day for me. I did not flip out on anyone and nobody took the brunt of one of my bad moods. These are the days that make taking all the medication I take worthwhile, and these are the days I dream of. On these days all I want to do is keep on living, and do not have any thoughts of death or me dying. I wonder what makes other people have good days. Is there anyone out there like me who feels that if they do not think about killing themselves than it is a good day? I just wonder about these things.

Chapter Fifteen

There is another type of manic phase that I go into. It is when I have voices in my head. They are not really voices, but rather characters from movies or television shows. For example, there is something about the movie *Good Will Hunting*. There are certain scenes from that movie that just replay over and over in my head. For instance, the scene where they are sitting in front of the river and Robin Williams is talking to Matt Damon about how he hasn't experienced real love or loss yet, that scene replays over and over in my head. It is quite frustrating. Also, there are scenes from the show *Friends* that tend to stick out in my mind, and just keep replaying. It might seem neat to some people, but to me it is extremely frustrating. I often think, "Why can't I just have a normal brain?"

The only time I hear voices are when I am extremely tired and depressed. I will hear things like, "You would be better up in heaven," or "Just take that knife and use it, come on do not be a chicken." Times like these I usually take something to help me fall asleep because if I do not, then the consequences could be awful. Many times driving home from the shore I would hear voices telling me just to put an end to my life. I would hear voices telling me that I would be better off dead. As I sit here writing this, I think about how absurd it all sounds. Of course it sounds absurd; I am not depressed right now. However, I am sitting here thinking about how I would definitely not be better off dead. My husband would be devastated, and so would my children and the rest of my family and friends. Also, I am eventually going to become a Certified Nursing Assistant, and those patients are going to need me. See, when I am stable like I am now, everything makes total sense. However, my world gets turned upside down when I am depressed or manic and I cannot see straight. It is almost like being intoxicated with faulty thinking, I think that is the best way I can describe it.

Trying to describe what it is like to have bipolar is not an easy feat. Personally, no two days are ever the same. There are days when I wake up and the last thing I want to do is get out of bed. I even get jealous if my husband is out of bed before I get up. I hear my kids in the background and that is what usually gets my ass out of the bed. If I am depressed though, this is such a struggle as I have described before.

Then I have days where the world seems a glow and I just cannot wait to start my day. Getting my kids dressed is not a chore, but something that comes as a pleasure to me. Making their breakfast is an honor and kissing my husband goodbye is not upsetting because I know I will see him again in about eight hours which go by quick most days. I happily take my son to school and am excited when I get to talk to the other parents or the teachers. It is fun to go to Dunkin Donuts and get myself coffee and two donuts and then drive home and watch some morning television. If only every morning could be like the one I just described I think my life would be close to perfect. However, that is not how a majority of the days go.

A majority of my mornings start with me struggling to get out of bed. "Why should I get out of bed?" is usually my first thought. I think this has something to do with the fact that I have not taken my medication yet. It is a struggle to get a shower, afterward which I tend to feel a little bit better. When I am depressed, it is also a struggle getting my two-year-old ready for the day. My four-year-old tends to get ready himself, only I have to give him breakfast. He can usually tell if I am feeling bad about myself because he will ask, "Are you okay Mommy?" I always reply with "Yes, I am fine." Unless I am crying, then I have to tell him that I am just a little bit sad today. Sometimes my depressed mood will lift pretty quickly after taking my medication and other times it lingers on throughout the day. This is something that I find quite frustrating; I wish the medication always worked. If I feel depressed than I honestly do not want to play with my children, and if I do, it is a struggle to get through. All I want to do when I feel this way is get under the covers and let the world pass me by, but that is not realistic. Life must go on, even if one feels depressed. I am sure many of you reading this have had times when you have felt blue, well to the bipolar person it is like feeling one-hundred times that feeling. If I simply felt blue than I could function much better, but it is not that way, it is like a cloud has come over me and I cannot escape.

Chapter Sixteen

People often ask me when I am honest with them and tell them that I am depressed, "What are you depressed about?" The truth is there is no specific thing that I am depressed about. Sure, if something happened to someone in my family, than there would be a reason. However, with bipolar disorder, it is not like that. There are no specific reasons as to why you can go from being happy-go-lucky to wanting to end your life. That is probably one of the worst things about the disorder is that it can strike out of nowhere. One minute you will be watching an interesting movie with your husband, the next you think about what a knife would feel like cutting across your skin. The fact that the disorder can be so random is what leads people to confusion. "But you were just laughing a minute ago" they will say. "I know, but now I am extremely depressed" I will tell them as they look at me with a face of surprise and confusion.

The disorder often goes the other way for me as well. I will become manic. There are several different things that may occur when I get manic. One thing is that I get extremely talkative, and I call all my friends in my phone book. Another thing that may happen as I discussed before is that I will have racing, repetitive thoughts in which I cannot get certain scenes from movies or television shows out of my head. Finally, there is the worst part of me being manic in which I have no fear about anything and I will drive down the shore and gamble because I think I have the magic secret on how to beat a machine. My manic phases are easier to diagnose. I am pretty good at hiding when I feeling depressed.

Hiding depression is one of the things I hate the most about this disorder. Nobody wants to be around someone who is down all the time, or some of the time, so I pretend like everything is okay. We will be driving to my in-laws and I will be feeling like shit, but I have to put a smile on my face. Do you have any idea how hard and painful this is? All I want to do on these occasions is go home and hide in my bed, but you cannot live your life like that. I am getting a little better at telling people that I am just feeling a little bit down. Hey, honesty is the best policy, as they say. It is just difficult for me to do this and I am not sure why. Even with my own parents I try to fake that I am feeling fine when I am not. There have been times when I have gone over there and have taken pills from their medicine cabinet hoping that it would make me feel better. Now I know better, but not at the time. My dad is always in a good mood so I even tried some of his epilepsy medication. Sounds absurd, I know, but anything to try to feel better.

The person that I am the most honest with about how I am feeling is my husband Dennis. In fact, there are times when I smile and he will say, "Trace, you do not have to smile just for me." He really is the best husband in the world. He can take one look at me and say, "You are feeling depressed aren't you?" He also knows if I am faking my mood when we go to social gatherings. In fact, sometimes he knows me too well. It would be nice if he did not know every time I was depressed because as I think, "Who wants to live with someone if they are either depressed or manic?" However, what I have to realize is that he truly does love me, faults and all, and it is not like I asked for this and he knows that I would get rid of it in a heartbeat if I could.

Chapter Seventeen

Moving on, it is time that I explain what has happened during this past month. It begins with me taking a trip down the shore. This trip, I had absolutely no regard for how much money I was spending. Unfortunately, I had the use of a credit card. I must have racked up almost $1,000.00 on this credit card and in addition I must have hit the ATM about six times. When I was down to my last twenty-five cents, I felt a tap on my shoulder and this person said, "Excuse me," and it was Dennis. He told me that my dad was with him and that they wanted me to go to the hospital. They had already called my doctor and he felt it would be a good idea if I spent a few days there. Seeing my dad there at the casino, I felt so ashamed. Had it really taken them driving all the way down the shore for me to finally realize that I had a problem? I think the answer is yes. I needed help, and I did not try to fight them at all either. I just went with Dennis in one car and my dad drove the car I had driven down in.

Despite my humiliation, there was a little feeling of relief. I did not realize it, but I was crying out for help. So, it was a long drive to the hospital that Dennis took me to. We even stopped to get McDonald's on the way there because we were both so hungry. I remember I had two cheeseburgers and a diet coke. Have to balance it out with the diet coke you know. Anyways, when we got to the hospital the first thing was that I went to triage where they took my vitals and gave me a pregnancy test. There was a chance I could be pregnant since we were trying and all, but obviously I was not.

After triage I was put into this little room for about an hour and a half. Talk about trying to make someone go crazy. They made me get into the hospital shirt and pants. I remember that it was freezing in that room and that one of the nurses was nice enough to get me a blanket. I got extremely depressed while sitting in that room. I began to take it out on Dennis because who else was I going to take it out on? I began yelling at him and the last thing I said before he walked out the door was, "I wish you were dead." See, I had not taken my medication that morning. I was at the casino throughout the whole night. So, my moods were everywhere. So, Dennis ended up leaving, and I cannot say that I blame him.

Looking back, that was not a good idea to put me in that small, confined room. I guess they had no choice because they were waiting for a bed to open up in the Crisis section of the hospital. However, I started to go a little bit crazy sitting in that room. I got hysterical and could not stop crying. People walking by would look in on me and think I was some sort of crazy person, and that is what I felt like. I think they should make people wait in large areas sort of like when you are waiting for a plane. But not in a small space, it just made me feel so trapped, as if I did not feel that already.

Finally a nice young woman from the Crisis Center brought me over to her section of the hospital. The room that they put me in had a bed so I could lie down and it was just a little more cozy. Initially, this worker, I am not sure if she was a nurse or what, asked me all sorts of questions. For example, "Do you feel like hurting yourself?" to which I actually answered truthfully and said, "yes." "Do you have a plan?" to which I told her I wanted to do it as painlessly as possible and just swallow a bunch of pills. "Do you hear voices?" she asked. I told her about the movies and television that replay over and over in my head. There were more questions, but I do not want to bore you. Basically, she felt and the head doctor of that wing felt that I was a danger to myself and that I should stay overnight for observation.

I was in that room until about one in the morning and then another young woman walked me upstairs. Again I had to answer a ton of questions and I do not think I got to bed until two in the morning. The beds were so uncomfortable, but that did not matter. What mattered was that I was stopped and forced to look at myself in the mirror. When you are in a hospital, there is really nothing to do but think. Think about your life, what brought you there, what you were going to do when you got out, etc. I was only in there for that one night, but boy did it change my life. I knew I never wanted to be hospitalized for this again and I never wanted to be that out of control again in my life.

When I went to my psychiatrist the following day, he prescribed Lithium for me and I can honestly say that the drug has changed my life. I do have to get blood work done every so often so that they can check the levels. Too much and you can get toxic. I am also on other things for anxiety: Abilify, Klonopin, and Effexor. I have to take these drugs every morning or my day is just pure hell. As my dad pointed out, just like a diabetic has to take insulin, I have to take my medication so that I am alright.

Something that is not easy to discuss but I think it helps show how difficult this disorder can be on family members is that during this time, I nearly got divorced from Dennis. This was after the whole shore ordeal. He was getting to a point where he just could not take it. Also, there were other reasons as well. I was talking excessively to someone that I had met online. This was something that I would do when I was depressed and lonely to try to feel better. However, this was the first time that it got more serious than just talking. This infuriated Dennis as it would probably any husband. I was not only talking online to this person, but on the phone as well. I would go to this person when I was upset, rather than Dennis. So, my shore trips, my depressive episodes and having an emotional relationship with someone else nearly cost me my marriage.

Dennis took three weeks off from work so that we could resolve this issue. His thing was that if we were getting divorced, he did not want to drag it out. After going back and forth numerous times on whether or not we were getting divorced we finally decided to stay together. It also helped that the Lithium was kicking in and working.

I want to point out that Dennis is the most supportive person I know but that there is only so far a person can go before they reach their breaking point. I do not blame Dennis for threatening divorce, after all I had done the same thing at times. He is only human and there is only so much a human can go through. I hope to God that now he feels a little bit better about my bipolar, as I think that he does. I also hope that this proves how damaging denial can be. I nearly lost my husband because I was refusing to admit that I had a problem.

Chapter Eighteen

My days now are not perfect, but they are as close to perfect as I believe they will get. Yes, I have gone gambling a few times since I have been on the right meds. However, I have never been out of control. The last time I went down the shore to gamble, the time my husband and dad came to pick me up, I had gone walking the streets for money. I could have been killed because I was in a very dangerous part of the city. I do not do things like that now. The worse it gets is that I will lose twenty or thirty dollars which still is not good, but I am not in a manic phase. I go down simply as someone who enjoys gambling. Hey, I never said I was perfect, and I know that I never will be. However, who is perfect? I have not met anyone that is yet.

The truth is if I stay on my meds and just keep talking it out, I will be okay. My mom always tells me to take it one day at a time and she is right. If I try to do more than that, I get overwhelmed. So, my plans for the future are to get my Certified Nurse Assistant diploma and work for a hospice. I volunteer for a hospice currently and absolutely love it. People think I am crazy, but I think there is something beautiful about being there for someone when they are dying. Now, many of you probably are thinking I am loony because someone dying is depressing. However, I tend to have a different view. How wonderful it is to be there with people towards the end of their life, how special is that? Also, it is an honor I think.

One lady who I volunteered for lived for about six months after our first visit together. She was so interesting and taught me a lot about life. I look back and think about just how special that time was that we spent together. I mean, here she was dying and could have been spending that time with anyone, but she chose to spend those hourly visits with me. What an honor. She sure was a fighter and that is what I think I learned from her, to have strength in this world despite adversity. She was great. She had outlived four husbands, had three children, and two dogs. It was sad to see her go, but I will never regret the time that we spent together, not one minute of it.

Currently, I visit an elderly gentleman who used to be a commercial pilot. Boy is he a pistol! He has taught not to take anything from anyone and to stand up for yourself. When they do not treat him right at the residence where he resides, he lets them know it! He also has a special heart and genuinely cares what is going to happen when he is gone to his three girls and one boy. What a special man. So anyways, it is taking care of the dying that I want to do for a living. I truly feel that it is my calling to do this line of work.

Chapter Nineteen

I should point out that there are things that help me feel better. For one, I love to write and have just gotten back into doing it. I write poetry and books and hopefully you will get to read some of my books someday. Also, being with my kids is very therapeutic for me. When I need to stop thinking about how I am feeling, I spend time with them or my husband. Also, going for long walks on sunny days is also very therapeutic. Doing my hospice is wonderful for my soul. I am not trying to say that these things will get me out of my darkest moods, but when I feel myself on the brink of a depressive episode, sometimes these things will take the edge off. Not always, but sometimes and it is important to try to fight these mood swings. My motto is that I will not let bipolar have the power over me if I can help it.

Something that is a challenge for me is going to therapy to talk out my problems and the issues I am facing. I have gone to several counselors for a couple visits and then terminated our relationships simply because I am uncomfortable talking about myself. Perhaps you are like that as well? You do not take any comfort in talking about yourself. However, despite my hesitation, I am going to have to force myself to enter some sort of therapy because they say that and staying on the right medication is what works best for the person with bipolar disorder. Sometimes to get better we have to do what we do not want to do. Another thing is that I am going to try to find a Gambler's Anonymous group to go to in order to get a grip on my gambling issues. Making these strides is so important for the healing of my soul. I need to make them in order to feel better in the long run. Fighting bipolar disorder is like a running in a long-distance race, it takes time to feel better to get to that finish line, as opposed to being a sprint and trying to feel better in a heartbeat.

If there is one thing I could get across to some of you is to not be in denial like I was for countless years. If you sense something is wrong with you then seek help. You know yourself the best. Maybe you will notice that you react very strangely to things, or that you feel like you can conquer the world, seek help. Perhaps life seems so bleak that it does not seem worth living, seek help. I could have prevented a lot of pain towards other people and pain that I myself experienced if I had just admitted that something did not seem right here. I do not sit here and look back with regret that gets you nowhere fast. Instead, I have learned from my past mistakes and look forward to my bright future. There is freedom that comes with admitting we have a problem, Some people think that they have to stay in this prison of depression and racing thoughts, but you do not. There is help out there and please do not be afraid to seek it.

It is worth mentioning that an important part of my life is my support system. You have to have people out there that you can call or go see when you are feeling down or when you are feeling manic. There are people out there that love you and want to help you and that is what you have to realize. Let those people into your hearts, do not shut them away. First and foremost my husband is my biggest supporter and fan. Also, I have two of the greatest parents on this planet. They are always there when I need them and I am blessed to have them and my husband in my life along with my terrific friends. Do not think like I did for many years that people will think you are a freak, if people love you, then they will love you despite your problems. Also, have safe places to go to when you feel like your mind is racing and you have to get out of the house. And I want to stress the word *safe*. Not somewhere like, oh, I do not know, a casino where there is the potential to get drunk for free and lose all of your money. I am talking more along the lines of a friend's house or maybe the library if you need quiet. Also, if you wake up in the middle of the night, do not hesitate to wake your spouse if you have one or call a good friend. Good friends will let you call at any hour. And just be honest with the person with how you are feeling.

In closing, this is my story and I am sure there are thousands if not millions just like it. The truth is my bipolar disorder could be a lot worse. Sure, it is a pain that I get depressed and I do some very risky things, but overall, I do not have it as bad as many people who suffer from this mental illness. Again, I am not looking for sympathy that is not my intention. As I said before I hope that more people come forth about this mental illness. It is not a weakness, it is a chemical imbalance that is treatable. For a long time, I think I was in denial because if I admitted something was wrong, then I was admitting defeat. If you have bipolar disorder, I recommend that you write about it, and get it out of your system. It has been tremendously therapeutic for me, and I am sure it will be for others who suffer with this mental illness. If you are reading this and have bipolar disorder, please know that you are not alone and that there is help out there and you can feel better! Finally, if you are reading this and love someone with this mental illness than hang in there, support them, and try to find them the right help. They might not thank you right away, but in the long run they will be grateful. I know that I am grateful for all those that have helped me along this roller-coaster ride called my life. But hey, life would be boring without a little adventure, right?

www.ingramcontent.com/pod-product-compliance
Lightning Source LLC
Chambersburg PA
CBHW030534290526
45786CB00004B/1714